Autonomous Employees In Leadership Roles

Workplace Gems For Management

Louis Bevoc

Published by
NutriNiche System LLC

Louis Bevoc books...simple explanations of complex subjects

Awareness

Introduction

Leaders are often thought of as individuals who are in charge of people, projects, and processes. They make decisions on important matters, provide guidance to the employees, and are not afraid to "step up to the plate" when needed. Workers depend on them to be there when someone stronger or more experienced is needed to handle problems that cannot be handled alone. Always at the forefront, leaders personify the norms and values of their organizations while putting in extra effort to assure those organizations' goals and objectives are accomplished.

All of the above thinking about leaders is correct and that is why they are valuable to the organizations that employ them. Their experience and skills are needed in many different situations to make the best decisions based on the circumstances that surround them. Without good leaders, organizations can quickly come to a standstill and even cease to exist if too many wrong decisions are made.

Unfortunately, leaders cannot be everywhere at the same time. Their skills and abilities might be needed for a particular problem, but they are somewhere else do the problem goes unsolved or, worse yet, a costly wrong decision is made. This lack of ubiquity is a major reason why leaders need good employees who work for them. Those employees need to work without supervision and assume a management role for their jobs. They are known as autonomous employees in leadership roles, and they are highly valued by the organizations that employ them.

Autonomous employees in leadership roles (referred to as autonomous employees for the remainder of this book) are unique. They have the ability to do many things that other employees cannot and do not need direct supervision to do so. They also take on management responsibilities without being classified as managers and they take an entrepreneurial approach when performing their jobs. However, they function more as intrepreneurs than entrepreneurs. Intrepreneurs and entrepreneurs have some similarities, but they also differ as shown below.

Entrepreneurs

- Start with a vision and build companies from the ground up with the intent of selling a product or service.
- Possess broad skills and abilities.
- Organization focused.
- Manage others.
- Motivated by organizational accomplishments.

Intrepreneurs

- Improve an existing product or service by exploring new opportunities.
- Possess specific skills and abilities.
- Job focused.
- Manage themselves.
- Motivated by job accomplishments.

As intrepreneurs, autonomous employees are sometimes required to think about different solutions to problems. This "thinking outside the box" is necessary for them to accomplish the goals of their jobs. For example, an autonomous landscape company salesperson might offer one free gutter cleaning if a potential customer signs a snow plowing and lawn cutting service contract. His landscape company does not offer gutter cleaning as a service, but the salesperson knows that the profit he makes off the lawn care and snow removal will be enough to cover one gutter cleaning, and his company has obtained a new customer.

In the above example, the salesperson acts in a leadership role because he makes a decision without his boss. His ability to think of something unique in order to get the sale is a bonus to the owner of his company. He also shows how he can take something from his job that already exists (the lawn care and snow removal service) and improve upon it for personal and organizational goal accomplishment.

Let's move forward into more discussion about the benefits of autonomous employees. These benefits show the value of these employees in everyday workplace situations and situations that present challenges for employees who do not possess the necessary skills to properly handle them.

Flexibility

Employees who are flexible are of great value to organizations because they are adaptable. The ability to adapt is important in many different workplace situations because it facilitates the implementation of new ideas and concepts. Without this implementation, organizations fail to grow and prosper; thereby causing all stakeholders (investors, owners, customers, suppliers, and employees) to suffer. Flexibility, however, is most important when it comes to change due to the challenges involved.

Unfortunately, change is extremely difficult for many people. In fact, it is so difficult for some individuals that they simply cannot handle it and refuse to accept it. They end up holding on to what they have and what they are used to because they do not want to leave their comfort zones. This refusal to accept something different is bad for employees and their employers because processes become obsolete and systems fail; thereby resulting in a meltdown of productivity and the demise of organizations. Autonomous employees are flexible, and this prevents disaster from striking due to their resistance to change.

Below are some of the challenges experienced by organizations that are undergoing change along with reasons why autonomous employees are not negatively impacted by those challenges.

Lack of employee acceptance

Employees often resist change. Some of the reasons for this include:

- *Fear of the unknown*

  One reason that people do not like to leave their established comfort zones is that they do not know what will happen. They are leaving familiar surroundings to venture into the unknown, and this makes them apprehensive.

  Apprehension also results from change in organizations because employees do not know what to expect in terms of their job responsibilities. They realize their jobs could get better...but they also know that they could get worse. This fear of the unknown causes them to resist leaving their comfort zones.

Fear of the unknown can be so extreme that some workers quit their jobs. They choose to abandon the situation completely rather than attempt to deal with the change. Autonomous employees do not fear the unknown and accept change rather than fight it.

- *Fear of job loss*

  Change often occurs because it makes processes and procedures more efficient. This is especially true for technological change. However, the downside to technological change is that it can eliminate jobs. Employees are aware of this threat, and they sometimes become a barrier to change because of it.

  Keep in mind that employees are not always terminated just because their jobs have been eliminated. Many workers move into other positions in the organization that require their skills. However, employees are not sure of what is going to happen so they fear that they might lose their jobs. For this reason, they resist change. Autonomous employees know their jobs are safe because of their value to management. They do not fear job loss and can, therefore, focus on doing their work to the best of their ability.

- *Fear of extra work*

Change can create more work for some employees, and this is something that they would prefer to avoid. This is especially true for when new customers are acquired. New customers often require work to meet their specific needs and demands, and that work falls into the laps of the employees. Organizations that grow do not always add personnel to keep up with that growth, and this increases the workloads of existing employees.

The extra work taken on by employees might only be temporary, but workers usually are not sure if this is the case. They fear that their new responsibilities will be permanent, and this will make their jobs more stressful. For this reason, they become a barrier to change. Autonomous employees do not fear extra work if it is going to make them better at their jobs.

Lack of management support

Management needs to support the change from start to finish, and this is not always the case. The following needs to be remembered in regard to management's involvement:

- *Start at the top*

  Typically management understands that change needs to start at the top of the organizational hierarchy. However, some leaders fail to understand the importance of their initial involvement. They have a few meetings and pass on the responsibilities to lower-level managers. Yes, they were initially involved...but the rank and file employees are not aware of that involvement. The workers only see their supervisor telling them about the change that is about to take place.

Employees need to see top leadership involved in change if they are expected to understand the importance. If they do not view the change as important, they could impede the process rather than helping it. Autonomous employees do not need leadership involved in order to accept change because they are able to accept it on their own.

- *Continual involvement*

This is an error that management makes on a regular basis. They implement the change and then move on to other job responsibilities. They completely remove themselves from the process and limit their involvement to occasional monitoring of the change progression. This does not work because it shows that management has no interest in seeing the change through. They are not dedicated to the overall process, and that lack of dedication trickles down to the rest of the employees.

Situations where management is not involved often produce poor results. Since none of the workers believe the change is important, it fails to be implemented. The change is then viewed as a failure, and this might not have been the case if management had been committed throughout the process. Autonomous employees are interested in seeing change take place because it helps their organizations, and they do not need continual involvement of management.

Lack of resources

Proper resources need to be available for organizations undergoing change. The following resources prevent challenges if they are scarce or not available:

- *Physical*

  Physical barriers involve space limitations. Some workplaces simply do not have the real estate necessary to make the change happen.

  For example, a toy manufacturing company might want to add a talking doll line to its production. The personnel can be hired, the funding is available, and the managers have the knowledge necessary to put the line into action. However, there is simply not enough room in the building to complete the process. The talking doll line needs 5000 square feet and the production area only has 1000 square feet available for use. In this case, the lack of space is a physical limitation that presents a challenge for the change.

  Autonomous employees find creative ways to work around space limitations. They rise up to the challenge, take the "bull by the horns," and move forward with completing their job tasks.

- *Mental*

    Sometimes change is unsuccessful because employees do not have the mental capacity to process it. In other words, they do not have the technical knowledge to see it through to completion. When this happens, "lack of knowledge" presents a challenge to the change.

    Organizations that recognize shortages of technical knowledge often hire people with the correct skills after the fact. However, this can result in a "too little, too late" scenario because the change has already failed. Autonomous employees have the technical knowledge to do their jobs so they are not affected by a lack of mental capacity during change.

- *Psychological*

    Employees might not be motivated to make the change because they do not view it as advantageous. They want to see the benefits they will receive, and many times those benefits are not clear. The only thing that is clear is the fact that their job will be made more difficult until they have made the necessary adjustments.

    Please note that the benefits employees are searching for do not have to be monetary. A pay raise is nice, but it is only a temporary solution. Workers want to know how the change will help them perform their jobs. In short, they do not want to change just for the sake of changing...especially when the process requires time and effort.

Autonomous employees realize that the benefits of change might not be immediate. They are able to visualize the positive impact down the line which motivates them to accept the change and complete their job tasks.

Lack of planning

Companies that fail to plan for change can run into many challenges. This planning needs to be for different time frames including:

- *Now*

  Organizations that are not properly prepared for change can experience problems. Their lack of planning can be a barrier to progress that prevents the change from taking place.

  An example of this type of situation is a grocery store that wants to generate sales in January by selling crab legs. The store has the cooler space available for this new item, and their personnel have the proper training and knowledge. They have also placed ads in local newspapers to attract customers. However, the refrigerated foods buyer does not realize that crab legs are not available for purchase at this time because orders need to be placed three months in advance due to limited supply. Ultimately, crab legs are not brought into the store, shelves remain empty, and customers are angry. In short, the lack of planning on the buyer's part was a barrier to the change.

Autonomous employees are always prepared for change so they are able to accept it when necessary.

- *Short-term*

Successful change can face barriers due to a lack of short-term planning. Consider the seafood example above, and assume the buyer is able to find crab legs to bring into the store. Within two weeks, demand exceeds expectations and more shelf space is needed for expansion. Unfortunately, additional shelf space is not available because there was no planning for this to happen. In this situation, a lack of short-term planning challenges the success of the change.

Autonomous employees plan for short-term changes so they are ready when those changes take place.

- *Long-term*

Similar to short-term planning, successful change can face barriers due to a lack of long-term planning. Again, consider the seafood example above. Assume things are running smoothly for nine months...until the holiday season approaches. Now, the store needs more shelf space for honey glazed spiral sliced hams because they sell well for holiday parties. However, the extra space is not available because the crab legs are using it. In this situation, a lack of long-term planning challenges the success of the change.

Autonomous employees plan for long--term changes so they are ready when those changes take place.

Lack of employee involvement

Employees need to be involved in change for it to be successful. This involvement includes the following aspects:

- *Process ownership*

    Process ownership takes root when employees take charge of their jobs and related tasks. They are able to function with limited supervision, and their work output exceeds expectations. The quality of their work also improves because they identify with their jobs and their organizations.

    Employees who want to feel truly involved in an organization can achieve that feeling through process ownership. Process ownership also helps workers accept change because they are interested in doing what is best for the organization. Based on this, a lack of process ownership can be a barrier to change. One of the major benefits of autonomous employees is their strong process ownership which helps them accept and embrace change.

- *Trust*

  Trust is critical for employee involvement. Workers who do not trust management do not want to be a part of organizational actions or decisions...and this includes anything related to change. In this respect, workers who do not trust management are a challenge to any type of change. Autonomous employees trust management and behave as a part of it; thereby helping them buy into the changes being made.

- *Identification*

  Employees who identify with their organization believe in that organization's actions and want to get involved. They see the organization as a reflection of themselves, and they want to see it succeed. For example, a man who spends his free time working with animal rescue groups identifies with his organization because they donate money to the local humane society.

  Workers who identify with their employer typically embrace change because they believe their organization is making the right choices. Lack of identification can be a barrier to change because that belief is missing. Autonomous employees identify with their employer which helps them accept change.

Lack of training

Training is important for successful change progression. This training can be conducted in various ways including:

- *Internal managers*

  Internal managers often make the best trainers because they understand the needs of the organization. These individuals tailor the training to fit the operation, and they eliminate unnecessary information that takes up time and clutters employees' minds. Autonomous employees do not need to be trained by internal managers because they are able to train themselves and accept change.

- *External consultants*

  Trainers from outside companies can be hired to educate workers on changes taking place. External consultants are advantageous because they are experienced trainers. They might not understand the specific needs of organizations, but know how to train employees with the information provided to them. Autonomous employees do not need to be trained by external consultants because they are able to train themselves and accept change.

- *Web-based*

Web-based training works well for skilled individuals and those who require limited supervision. This is a very cost-effective method because fewer resources are required. Also, if the training is not live, employees can learn at their convenience with the option to return to any area that they do not understand. Autonomous employees are believers in web-based training and they use it to help them accept change.

Now you understand why flexibility, especially when it comes to change, is an advantage of having autonomous employees. Let's move forward to a discussion on innovation, the next benefit of employing these workers.

Innovation

What exactly is innovation? Is it thinking of new ideas? Is it developing novel products and services? Is it designing better processes? Actually, it involves all of the above. Innovation adds something of value to an organization. This value can be internal or external, and it is often complex because it cannot always be defined by a single event. For example, product development often involves testing different prototypes in different markets to find where there is consumer demand. If a new product is scrapped because it did not work in the first market it was tested in, then there is no innovation...there is only an idea.

Some people confuse creativity with innovation. They are linked, but they are not the same. Creativity is the process of associating thoughts and ideas with each other in order to create something that is potentially useful for an organization. Innovation is fueled by creativity in the workplace.

Innovation is the process of putting creativity into action and adding value to an organization. Creativity needs innovation in order to be useful in the workplace.

People also confuse invention with innovation. Again, they are related to each other, but they are not the same. Invention is the process of creating something that never existed in the past. Innovation is fueled by invention in the workplace

Innovation is the process of putting invention into action and adding value to an organization. Invention needs innovation in order to be useful in the workplace.

Some innovation seems to be based on good fortune. For example, an advertising agency might use an artist's song for a successful car commercial. However, without the advertising agency's background and experience, the value of the music would likely not have been recognized. Usually, there is a significant amount of effort behind all innovation.

In short, innovation adds something of value to the workplace. It harnesses creativity and makes it useful for an organization. It is related to creation and invention, but they are not the same. Some innovation appears to be serendipitous, but it usually stems from employees' hard work.

In order for innovation to be truly beneficial, it needs to be an active part of every aspect of an organization. Some people believe it only applies to new product or service launches, but this is not the case.

Innovation is important for manufacturing, distribution, sales, marketing, customer service, etc. because customers demand things easier, faster, cheaper, and better than ever before. The only way to meet these demands is to make improvements through innovative thinking.

Autonomous employees are on the front lines of innovation because they are always trying to improve themselves and their work. They add value to their organizations because their knowledge, effort, and attitude result in excellent job performance. In terms of innovation, the worth of these employees cannot be underestimated because they are inherently wired to find ways of making their jobs more effective and efficient.

Below are some significant benefits offered by innovation along with supporting workplace examples involving autonomous employees.

Increased productivity

Innovation drives people to work harder, and that is why innovative organizations have more productive employees. Companies that are constantly looking to implement ideas and concepts need more from their employees, and those employees rise up to the occasion because they see the end results.

Organizational example

Ricky works in quality assurance at a waste recycling company. His company is very committed to new technology because they want to grow and capture more of the market share. Candice, the president, is very involved with this task. She makes sure that technological advances are tested in every area of the facility. This week, she is trying a new sorting machine that is faster and more accurate when separating different types of waste.

Ricky likes the fact that the waste recycler is innovative because it makes his job easier and more defined. When something new is being tested, he goes "above and beyond" his job requirements to make sure he thoroughly investigates every aspect related to quality.

The innovation at the waste recycler drives Ricky to work harder at his job. His output increases and this increase is beneficial for the organization. Ricky is a good example of an autonomous employee who is functioning in a leadership role.

Increased motivation

The explanation for this benefit is fairly simple and straightforward. People are inspired to work for innovative organizations because they like being involved in projects that are new or different. Novel ideas and concepts are constantly being put into action, and this motivates employees to do their jobs to the best of their ability.

Organizational example

Jane has worked as a distribution manager for a convenience store chain for the past 13 years. Distribution works on very low-profit margins, so the company is always searching for competitive advantages. The CEO believes these advantages are best discovered through innovation. He encourages all employees to put their thoughts and ideas into action in an attempt to make the organization more efficient and effective.

Jane likes the innovative aspect of the convenience store chain. Her job is enjoyable because the company is always attempting new ideas for distribution. They are currently experimenting with drones to see if they can expedite deliveries of certain products. This is truly exciting, and it inspires Jane to do her best.

Jane's motivation stems from the innovation of the convenience store chain, and this is beneficial for her and the company. By doing her best, Jane is an autonomous employee.

Increased creativity

As mentioned in the introduction, creativity fuels innovation. However, if that creativity is not put into action, then it is wasted. This type of waste is not likely to happen in innovative organizations because they have people who are qualified to ensure ideas are put into action. This does not guarantee success, but it assures creators that their ideas will be taken to the next level.

In short, employees that work for innovative organizations are more likely to be creative because they know their ideas will be followed through on. This gets creative juices flowing and opens doors to new ways of thinking.

Organizational example

Rafael is an engineer for an automotive manufacturer. His job is to find ways to reduce the costs of building cars without jeopardizing quality or safety. Recently, he designed a new airbag that has the same strength as existing airbags, but requires 12 percent less material to manufacture. Executives at the plant like Rafael's idea, and they immediately test it on four different types of vehicles.

Rafael does not yet know the results of the testing, but he is motivated by the fact that his work is appreciated and taken seriously. This inspires him to work harder on other projects and it also makes him an autonomous employee. His creative juices are flowing because he knows his ideas will be put into action.

Increased competitiveness

Consumers purchase products and services in order to make their lives easier. The internet has made them more informed than they ever were in the past and it also gives them a variety of options. Innovation gives organizations an advantage because it keeps them on the cutting edge and ahead of the competition.

Organizational example

Charlotte is the CEO of a razor company named Remedol that targets women for sales of their products. The competition in the women's razor industry is fierce, and Remedol is not one of the bigger players. They do not have the same advertising and marketing money available as the larger companies, so they have to find other ways to compete. Charlotte strongly believes that competition is best accomplished through innovation.

Recently, a Remedol research and development employee named Ronnie came up with a new idea for a razor. The contour is made to fit women's legs and the razor is enlarged to make it easier to shave hamstrings and calves. Charlotte was ecstatic about this creation and immediately added it to the company's product line.

After only two months, Remedol's sales increased by five percent. Innovation led to the new razor's success, and it gave the company a competitive advantage. Ronnie's inspiration for the new razor idea truly makes him an autonomous employee.

The above examples show that autonomous employees are valuable for innovation in organizations. They understand what they need to do and are motivated to do so without help or direction from their boss. The next section discusses another benefit of employing autonomous employees known as logical thinking

Logical thinking

People who are logical thinkers use reasoning to make decisions. This reasoning develops from their knowledge and experience and it is used to determine what could or should happen under the given circumstances. Without the skill to think logically, people's decision-making is hindered and they typically do not make the best choices.

Unfortunately, many employees in workplaces do not think logically. They make decisions based on guesswork and emotions which impairs their decision-making. Poor decisions affect their job performance and, worse yet, they impact their organizations in a negative manner which is why business leaders put decision making abilities at the top of their list when hiring people for or promoting people to top positions.

Autonomous employees have the ability to think logically. Quite simply, if they did not have this ability, then they would not be considered autonomous by the top people in their organizations. They have specific skills that allow them to analyze situations pertaining to their jobs and make good decisions. Some of these skills are listed and described below for a better understanding of how and why autonomous employees are logical thinkers who provide value to workplaces.

Analysis skills

This might be the most important skill of logical thinking because it provides clarity for employees. Autonomous employees use their analysis skills to break things down for simplification and easier understanding. In other words, they are able to take something that is complex and turn it into something basic so it can be easily comprehended.

Analysis skills are extremely valuable when autonomous employees are involved in problem-solving. They break down the problem into manageable pieces and analyze each piece separately. This process helps them make better decisions, but it also helps their coworkers because those coworkers' understanding of the problem is simplified; thereby increasing their chances of resolving the problem if their involvement is needed.

An example of the analysis skills possessed by autonomous employees involves a woman named Beth who works for a bicycle manufacturing plant. She is responsible for making sure a certain brand of 10-speed bicycle is available in retail bike shops in 37 states within eight weeks. To do this, Beth breaks the United States into four districts including the North-East, North-West, South-East, and South-West. For each district, she finds a distributor who has an established base of bike retail stores that they deliver to on a weekly basis. This distribution network reduces Beth's job responsibilities dramatically and allows her to focus on four distributors rather than hundreds of retail bike stores. It also makes it easier for any of Beth's coworkers to fill in for her if she is absent or moves on to another position.

Assessment skills

Autonomous employees are able to make accurate judgments about happenings that concern their jobs. They do this by determining what is relevant and what is not relevant and understanding what is being said or written. The decisions made from these judgments are more often right than wrong due to their assessment skills.

An example involving the assessment skills of autonomous employees is the application of legal documents to job tasks that they are performing. These individuals are not attorneys, but their superior reading comprehension and extensive experience in their line of work allow them to understand what is written and decide on the best course of action. They are able to identify relevant information in the material and use it for decision-making purposes. However, if they are unsure of what is written after reading a document, then they are smart enough to reach out to others who can provide them with the help necessary to gain an understanding of the subject matter.

Resourcefulness skills

Autonomous employees realize the value of resources and conserve those needed for their jobs. They avoid waste by simply using less or becoming creative with the resources they have on hand. An example of creativity is their tendency to print fewer documents then their coworkers, choosing instead to save the paper and ink needed to print physical copies of what is already on their computer screen.

The resourcefulness skills exhibited by autonomous employees are beneficial in two different ways. First, their organizations benefit in cost savings because less money is spent replacing depleted stock and supplies. Second, this resourcefulness is seen by others; hereby creating a precedent in the workplace. Other employees follow the lead and also begin to conserve which leads to organization-wide cost savings.

Action skills

Autonomous employees are action-based because they take charge of all aspects of their jobs. They do not sit back and let work build as they contemplate their next move. They strongly believe in getting a jump on the tasks they need to complete so they do not end up short of time later on.

Autonomous employees are proactive as opposed to reactive. They have the mentality that "an ounce of prevention is worth a pound of cure" so they can prevent something from happening rather than repair the damage it does after it has occurred.

Autonomous employees also take action when problems occur rather than waiting for the potential fallout. In short, they believe that "the first loss is the best loss" in situations that could grow into bigger problems if nothing is done. For example, they rewrite emails that might be somewhat vague rather than take their chances and send them out to the intended recipients. The emails might be understood by the recipients, but the potential for bigger problems down the line causes them to put in the extra time and effort to assure clarification.

Autonomous employees possess the above skills, and they use those skills to think logically. They analyze phenomena to draw conclusions, design strategies, make decisions, and take action. Logical thinking is critical for the growth and development of organizations, and it often stems from autonomous employees.

Commitment

The best workers are often those who are the most committed to the goals, values, and objectives of the organizations that employ them. Quite simply, they believe in what the organization is doing, what it stands for, and why it exists. They also share a vision with workplace leaders about the future of their organization and they will make sacrifices to assure that vision is achieved.

Unfortunately, employees who fit the mold of the above paragraph are few and far between due to the time and effort required to become committed. However, autonomous employees possess many of these traits which is another reason that they are thought of so highly by organizational leaders. Better yet, these workers are self-motivated and do not need help from people at the top to take ownership of the jobs; thereby becoming committed to the values and visions of their employers.

The motivation of autonomous workers can be explained by the *Goal Setting Theory*. This theory is explained below for a better understanding of its meaning and application to autonomous employees.

Goal-Setting Theory

This theory was developed by psychologist Edwin Locke, and it is one of the most widely known and respected theories in organizational psychology. Locke's work helped people understand motivation at work and job satisfaction, and it has been applied in a variety of different situations.

In short, Locke thought employees should set difficult and specific goals, and those goals would lead to higher work performance. This theory challenges the idea that employees should simply "do their best" since that type of thinking does not motivate people to perform optimally. Autonomous employees fit the theory well because they challenge themselves to learn new things and achieve higher goals.

Application in an organization

Becky is an autonomous employee who works as a loan officer at a major bank. Her job is to entice people to take out mortgages and equity loans through the bank. Typical loan officers at the bank write loans for five to seven new customers per month, but Becky has a goal to sign ten new customers a month for the next year.

She works tirelessly to accomplish her goal, sometimes staying at her desk until 9:00 pm to call customers after they get home from work. Customer response is slow at first, but eventually, word-of-mouth spreads that Becky is a great loan officer. Within a few months, people start calling her instead of her calling them.

Over the next year, Becky's hard work pays off as she picks up over 130 new customers. This accomplishment was very challenging, but she was successful because she was motivated by her goal. The goal was a difficult one, but it inspired her to give an effort above and beyond that of the average loan officer.

Becky's work ethic adheres to the premise of the goal-setting theory. Her efforts are beneficial to her own career and the financial well-being of the bank. In short, she is seen as a major asset by her bosses.

The above example shows how autonomous employees raise the bar in terms of their own expectations; thereby benefiting themselves and their organizations. However, goal setting is not the only variable that influences commitment. It also requires a positive attitude and persistence, both of which are discussed below for a better understanding of what they entail and what type of impact they have in the workplace.

Positive attitude

Without going into too much detail, attitude in the workplace refers to the way employees think about the various situations that they encounter while performing their jobs. It is a psychological state of mind that can fluctuate based on what is happening at the specific times, and it can be positive, negative, or somewhere in between.

Attitudes are psychological, but they lead to physical changes. In workplaces, they influence the behavior of employees which subsequently impacts the way they perform their jobs. Positive attitudes typically result in employees doing their jobs more effectively and efficiently while negative attitudes have the opposite effect.

Positive attitudes also make work more enjoyable for employees and they tend to complain less than their coworkers who have negative attitudes. Autonomous employees work hard to maintain positive attitudes so they tend to like their jobs and do them complaining. Their ability to always look at the bright side, along with their upbeat nature and hard work ethic, make them a pleasure to work around and supervise.

Autonomous employees with positive attitudes truly are gems in the workplace...especially since their managers cannot control all of the workplace factors that negatively influence those attitudes. An example of the influence that a positive attitude has on commitment is shown below.

Application in an organization

Roberta is an autonomous employee with a positive attitude who works as a cashier at a grocery store. She treats customers politely, focuses on their needs, and engages in upbeat conversations. Her positive attitude makes her job much more enjoyable and it increases her commitment to her employer. This attitude also helps the store owners with their business because the well-treated customers consistently return to purchase their groceries.

The above example shows how autonomous employees use their positive attitudes to help themselves and their employers. Now, let's look at the other variable that influences commitment known as persistence.

Persistence

The definition of persistence is not the same for everyone and it often depends on the situation. For example, a basketball player who persistently works at his game so he can get into the starting lineup is typically seen as positive while that same man's persistence in attempting to date his best friend's wife is usually seen as negative.

Persistence is considered to be positive for the purposes of this book and its relationship with commitment. Autonomous employees are persistent because they are motivated to achieve professional goals and objectives. They share the same vision as the leaders of their organizations and they take ownership of their jobs. They strive for effectiveness and efficiency; thereby making their jobs much more than just a way to make money and earn a living.

As noted earlier, autonomous employees are motivated and, as such, have positive attitudes about their jobs and their employers. These traits bring about natural persistence as they try to be the best they can be while helping their organizations grow and prosper.

Autonomous employees understand that persistence will help them become better at their jobs; thereby helping them achieve greater success in their careers. They have a keen sense of knowing when they are on the right path and continually reach for the "pot of gold" at the end. This effort takes more than just hard work. It also involves a vision to see what will result in terms of achieving their own and their organizations' goals.

Autonomous employees also realize that persistence can be the difference between success and failure. It does not completely guarantee that they will reach the goals they have set for themselves, but it does guarantee that their failure to achieve those goals will not be from lack of effort.

It can be said with confidence that persistence strengthens commitment. It requires determination, desire, and stamina, but autonomous employees know that the end result will be worth the time and effort that they have invested.

An example of persistence and its positive impact on commitment is shown below.

Application in an organization

Richard is a civil engineer in a construction company. He is an autonomous employee who is always striving to get better at his job. He knows of a computer program that will reduce the amount of work he does when working on bridges, but it costs $20,000 to purchase and implement due to the software cost and necessary training.

This cost of the computer program has prevented the owners of the company from purchasing it. However, their resistance does not stop Richard from continually pursuing it. He knows this program will make his job easier and save the company if he can convince the owners to buy it.

After six months of preaching the importance of this software, the owners decide to purchase it. They base their decision on the benefits touted by Richard, and they are convinced that the payback will be significant.

The new software increases Richard's commitment to the construction company, and this would not have happened without his persistent push for its purchase.

The above example shows how persistence is related to commitment. Let's move forward the next benefit of autonomous employees known as awareness.

Awareness

Awareness is probably the most wide-open benefit of autonomous employees because there is so much involved. It includes awareness of people, jobs, work environments, workplace cultures, leadership styles, management philosophies, and many other aspects of organizations.

Awareness, both of self and others, is important for employees because it helps them identify what they do best, what they need to improve on, where they are presently, and where they want to be in the future. Since autonomous employees are high on the awareness scale, they understand their strong and weak points and they know where they are and where they want to be. These realizations eliminate the uncertainty that many other employees have about their jobs and careers, and they make the jobs of workplace leaders less difficult.

The biggest benefits of the awareness possessed by autonomous employees include their ability to handle conflict, work with others, and control emotions. Each of these abilities is discussed below for a better understanding of what they entail.

Handle conflict

Autonomous employees are typically very good at handling conflict for two distinct reasons. One reason is that they simply avoid it. They have the ability to accurately read situations and know when conflict is precipitating and, when they can, they walk away from it. The second reason is they avoid becoming verbally aggressive when they are involved in conflict. This avoidance is not based on luck or natural tendencies...it is a learned skill that takes time to master.

Verbal aggressiveness is an important topic that warrants discussion because it minimizes or prevents conflict and the emotional stress that typically accompanies it. In the mid-1980s, Dominic Infante and C.J. Wigley defined verbal aggressiveness as a destructive form of communication involving an attack on the personal beliefs or self-concepts of others. At the time, that definition was based mostly on studies involving interpersonal relationships. Today, it can be applied to workplace relationships.

Unfortunately, verbal aggressiveness occurs in workplaces all over the world. The type of organization or industry sometimes plays a role in the amount that occurs, but it is virtually impossible to find a workplace where employees have never experienced any type of verbally aggressive behavior by their coworkers.

Employees use verbal aggressiveness for many reasons including lack of argumentative skills, trying to be humorous, being mad or in a bad mood, trying to appear "tough," and compliance gaining purposes. Regardless of the reason, these attacks send a negative message and the effects are rarely positive which is why autonomous employees are careful to avoid it.

Each of these reasons is examined in more details as follows:

Lack of argumentative skills

Contrary to what some people believe, arguing has some benefits. It allows people to express their viewpoints and hear the viewpoints of others. People who are able to "swallow their pride" can learn a lot from arguing, and they can apply that knowledge to future situations for constructive resolution of problems.

Swallowing one's pride, however, is often easier said than done....and this is why many people have difficulty arguing. The emotions they experience during arguments make them feel uncomfortable, and they have difficulty expressing their viewpoints without fumbling for words. They say things that they do not really mean...and they end up appearing under-informed or clueless while defending their positions.

Employees who have difficulty arguing sometimes resort to alternative methods for getting their point across. They raise their voice because they believe this strengthens their position, or they walk away indicating that their opponent is not worthy of their time. These methods do little to resolve the actual problem, and they typically are not effective.

A far worse combat strategy used by employees who lack arguing skills involves personally attacking their opponents. They mock people's physical appearance, past accomplishments, thoughts, beliefs, or ideas. This does nothing for defending positions, and it is offensive to the people who are being attacked, which is why autonomous employees avoid personal attacks.

Organizational example

Travis is a production supervisor at a brewery. He has been with the company for nine years, with the last three being spent in his current position.

One of Travis' bottling lines is stopped by the quality assurance manager Janice because the beer that does not meet the company requirement for color. This upsets Travis, and he tells Janice that her action is not justified. Janice calmly explains that the color of the beer is not right, and the line can be restarted after this issue is corrected. Travis believes the color is acceptable, and he becomes irate.

Rather than involving herself in a heated argument, Janice says she will get the color speciation chart from the laboratory to support her action. Instead of arguing his position on the matter, Travis tells Janice that quality assurance personnel are a total waste of money. He says that they work against the best interests of the company, and their department should be eliminated.

Without saying a word, Janice walks away and gets the plant manager so he can make a decision on the color of the beer. The plant manager supports Janice, and the line is stopped until the color of the beer complies with company specifications.

In this situation, Travis attacked Janice and her department because he did not have a legitimate argument for his belief that beer was the right color. Ultimately, his action created a relationship issue between himself and Janice, and it did nothing to defend his position.

Autonomous employees have the ability to argue and use this ability to avoid verbally aggressive personal attacks.

Trying to be humorous

Unfortunately, some people think it is funny when they attack others personally. In workplaces, employees who attack other employees often have an audience of coworkers present that they believe are being "entertained." People witnessing the verbally aggressive behavior might laugh, but usually, this is because they are uncomfortable. However, people being targeted by the verbal aggressiveness find absolutely no humor in the situation.

Organizational example

Serena is the paint department manager at a retail superstore. She employs five high school students in her department, and she makes it a point to make fun of them in front of other employees. She jokes about them being kids and their inability to perform simple job tasks without direct supervision.

Some of Serena's coworkers laugh at her comments, but this is mainly because they feel uncomfortable. They like the high school students and believe they are trying their best to do their jobs...but they also want to show that they have a sense of humor.

The high school students, however, do not find Serena's derogatory comments funny at all. They might not be seasoned employees, but they are not children, and they believe they are capable of completing tasks on their own.

Ultimately, Serena's verbal aggressiveness has a negative impact on the employees in the organization. She believes she is entertaining coworkers with her humor, when in fact she is offending some of them and creating discomfort for others.

Autonomous employees understand the boundaries of humor and use caution not to overstep those boundaries.

Being mad or in a bad mood

Everyone experiences bad moods. This is completely normal because things do not always go as people hope or plan, and negative emotions can surface. Unfortunately, those negative emotions can build in people to the point where they react in some type of hostile manner...including verbally attacking others.

Employees who are in bad moods sometimes take out their frustration on their coworkers by saying hurtful things that inflict psychological pain. This is bad because people say things that they do not really mean...but the damage is done, and it is difficult to reverse.

Organizational example

Jeremy is a construction supervisor. He and his wife always eat breakfast together before they both go to work. This morning, however, they get into an argument over finances at the breakfast table. Jeremy believes his wife spends too much money on unnecessary things, and she disagrees with him.

Jeremy shows up for work in a bad mood due to the argument with his spouse. At the first job he visits, he finds that his employees have made a mistake on the driveway they are pouring for a customer. They mistakenly poured five inches of cement instead of the agreed-upon four inches, and this means the job will not be profitable.

Jeremy is angry about this mistake, and he starts yelling at his employees. He calls them stupid and incompetent and tells them they should all be fired for making such a dumb mistake. The workers are demoralized and begrudgingly go back to doing their jobs.

Jeremy has been in the construction business for over 20 years, and he has seen this same mistake made in the past. He knows that this job will not be profitable, but it will not lose money for the company. His verbal aggressiveness resulted from the bad mood he was in due to the confrontation he had with his wife. Unfortunately, his words demotivated his employees and damaged his relationship with them.

Autonomous employees, like all employees, experience bad moods. However, they understand the damage they can cause by allowing those moods to spill out into verbal attacks.

Trying to appear "tough"

Some employees think that their verbal aggressiveness makes them appear stronger or tougher than others. They believe their language will prevent others from taking advantage of them or "stepping on their turf."

Employees who implement verbally aggressive strategies for toughness have thought about the psychological harm they are doing to others. This differs from being mad or in a bad mood because the hurt is intended and those inflicting the pain really do mean what they say.

Organizational example

Albert is a welder at a metal fabrication shop. He likes to do stainless steel welding, and he does everything in his power to make sure he gets assigned to the stainless jobs without the help of any other employees.

One of Albert's ways to prevent other employees from working on stainless steel projects is to attack their ability to do the job. Stainless steel welding requires special skills, and Albert has those skills. Other employees also have the skills, but they are not as talented as Albert...and he makes sure he lets them know it.

Albert makes fun of the other employees by laughing at the jobs they have completed. He tells them that they do not have the knowledge or skills to be stainless steel welders, and they should stick to the easier jobs to avoid getting fired for incompetence.

Albert's verbal aggressiveness results from him attempting to appear "tough." He likes doing stainless steel welding, and he wants everyone else to stay away from any projects involving it...so he attacks his coworker's ability to properly perform their jobs.

Autonomous employees are secure in their jobs and do not fear other employees getting involved with their work. In fact, they welcome these employees and treat them with respect so they can get more out of them in terms of help and productivity.

Compliance gaining purposes

Compliance gaining occurs when employees attempt to get coworkers to comply with their desires, wishes, or demands. Skillful employees do this using tactfulness and diplomacy. However, workers who are unable or unwilling to be tactful or diplomatic, often resort to verbally aggressive language to gain compliance.

Threats are a form of verbal aggressiveness used for compliance gaining purposes. Specifically, employees threaten coworkers in order to control them...with the fear of consequences for not meeting demands.

Threats have successfully changed employees' behavior in some instances, but other times they simply do not work. This is due to the fact that threats are only successful if the worker making the threat is willing to follow through if demands are not met. If threatening personnel are tested and fail to follow through, then the threat was unsuccessful.

Unfortunately, some people never test out the willingness of another employee to follow through on a threat...and this causes them to live under the control of that employee. Older employees, for example, often "bluff" younger employees into performing their job function in a certain manner based on the threat that failure to do so will result in disciplinary action. The younger employees never think to question the older employees because of their experience, so the bluff works well.

However, this bluff is only successful as long as the younger employees continue to believe it is true. If they find it to be false, the result may be a verbally aggressive conflict due to the feelings of victimization by the younger employee. If this is the case, then verbally aggressive behavior (the threat of consequences) leads to more verbally aggressive behavior...and the end result is a dysfunctional organization.

Organizational example

Claudia is a nurse at a hospital. She works in the Intensive Care Unit, and she does not like other nurses to make any changes to her patients' care requirements without first getting her approval.

To accomplish her objective, Claudia threatens the other nurses. She tells them that any nurse who makes changes to her patients' care will be disciplined by the head nurse. She states that the head nurse only allows doctors and Claudia to makes changes to her patients' care.

In reality, Claudia's threat is not true. Other nurses will not be disciplined for making changes to her patients' care requirements as long as they follow proper hospital protocol. However, Claudia's bluff works because none of the other nurses call her out on it. In other words, her threat is successful for compliance-gaining purposes.

Autonomous employees avoid threatening others because they know that this can lead to many other problems. They believe in opening lines of communication to gain compliance rather than making threats that they might not be able to follow through on.

Work with others

A major part of working with others involves understanding the culture of the organization. Autonomous employees understand the cultures of their organizations and they know how to work within those cultures.

In organizations, culture is made up of experiences, philosophies, protocols, behaviors, norms, and values that provide behavioral guidelines for employees. It starts at the top of the organizational hierarchy and works its way down into the rank and file. Employees can help establish behaviors and norms, but they do not have the same power as those in the upper levels of the established hierarchy. Top ranking members are the only people who have the authority, influence, and control needed to create the overall culture of the organization.

Autonomous employees' acute sense of awareness allows them to understand that every culture is distinctive based on the characteristics of the organization. They know that culture describes an organization and is created by the most influential members, and can be challenging to change. Armed with this knowledge, they know that they must behave in certain ways to get others to work with them and perform their jobs at peak levels.

Culture has a significant impact on many different aspects of organizational behavior including communication. Employees need to communicate in order to accomplish tasks and achieve organizational goals. This can be done verbally (talking, presentation, speeches, videos, etc.) or non-verbally (body language, pictures, signs, symbols, written words, etc.), but it all falls under communication. Autonomous employees realize that good communication keeps organizations healthy, while poor communicating is capable of destroying it.

Control emotions

Emotional control is important in many workplace situations because it prevents those situations from getting out of control. Autonomous employees are able to control their emotions while understanding the feeling of others and, as such, display high levels of emotional intelligence.

Emotional intelligence is a term that was developed by psychologists Peter Salovey and John Mayer, and later popularized by psychologist Daniel Goleman. Essentially, Goleman designated five major components of emotional intelligence. These components are:

Self-awareness

This refers to recognizing one's own feelings. People who are self-aware are able to identify and monitor their own emotions for control. These people are confident and have a good sense of humor. They are also aware of how they are perceived by others.

Self-regulation

This refers to controlling reactions or impulses. People who react quickly often end up saying things that they would not have said if they thought about the situation. Self-regulation makes people conscientious about what they are saying, and it prevents them from responding in ways that elevate the negativity of conversations.

Motivation

This refers to self-motivation for self-improvement. It goes above money and status (external rewards) by focusing on things such as satisfaction and happiness (internal rewards). It also includes a strong drive to accomplish goals and objectives regardless of the circumstances. Optimism is critical here...even when faced with potential failure.

Empathy

This refers to understanding other people's situations and taking a genuine interest in those situations. It often involves "walking a mile in another person's shoes" to fully comprehend their behavior and reactions. This is the most skillful component because it sometimes requires the anticipation of other's needs so the appropriate response can be made.

Social skills

This involves picking up on social cues to build relationships and work toward a common goal. It requires active listening and appropriate responding to persuade others and gain their trust. It also involves team-building and collaboration as a method of working with others.

Autonomous employees hear what others are saying and react emphatically without being upset or distraught. They know what their emotions are capable of doing, and they harness their feelings to prevent negative reactions from others. This type of behavior is beneficial in organizations because it prevents situations from becoming emotionally charged. Based on this, it is understandable why autonomous employees hold important positions in organizations.

One benefit of the awareness of autonomous employees that is often overlooked involves the receiving of information. More specifically, it involves their understanding of the pitfalls of too much information. They know that if they have too much information to process, then they will experience negative effects of what is commonly referred to as information overload.

Information overload is a phenomenon that is increasingly gaining attention in the workplace. In the business world, people are fed so much information that it is virtually impossible to keep track of it all. Prior to the 1980s, this information had to be written down by hand or remembered because personal computers were not typically found on employees' desks. When computers became common in organizations, their memory and storage made it much less difficult to store information and retrieve it when necessary. So this book can end now....correct? Unfortunately, it is not that simple because the amount of information that people try to absorb keeps increasing; thereby making it more difficult to store and retrieve. Add to this the explosion of the internet, and it is quite obvious to most people that there is simply too much information to keep track of in business.

When employees have too much information to process, they experience information overload. Information overload was a term made famous in 1970 by Alvin Toffler. However, Toffler could never have envisioned the impact the internet would have on this concept or the importance it would have for people in business all over the world. Employees simply do not have the ability or desire to process all of the information available to them, and this affects the ways they perform their jobs and the decisions they make at work.

When Toffler wrote about Information overload, it was a concept that was only found in academia. It was reserved for discussion among college professors in the soft sciences, rarely venturing out into the business world where it could take root with the general public. Technology changed this restriction, and information overload has never since been thought of as being limited to college campuses. People use the term regularly, and it is understood by virtually everyone.

While Toffler popularized the concept of information overload, he was not the first to notice its effects. In the early-to-mid-1900s, scientists studied this phenomenon as it related to the changes being experienced by people in society. Specifically, German sociologist Georg Simmel noticed the negative effects it had on people as the cities they lived in rapidly became modern and industrialized. He found these people had so much information thrown at them in short time periods that they were unable to react and cope. Their behavior showed signs of duress and confusion as they failed to adapt to the situations thrust upon them.

Later on, Simmel's observations were expanded upon by Jacob Jacoby, Donald Speller, and Carol Kohn Berning. These researchers conducted an experiment that bombarded the subjects with information about product brands, and they found that information overload led to poorer decision making. This research was not conducted on employees in organizations, but its finding had some application in business settings.

Fast forward to the 21st century, and the term information overload is now a household name. It is understood, in one form or another, by the masses and is even worthy of mention on cable news and late-night talk shows. In business, information overload is a common complaint of employees, regardless of the fact that it is not completely understood by those who complain about it. Unfortunately, this complaining is not going to stop because the world is fast becoming a global marketplace. More and more information is being shared via web-based sources on an instantaneous basis, and it is simply too much for most humans to process....so information overload results.

Like other workers, autonomous employees are subject to information overload when too much information comes their way. However, unlike other workers, their awareness of the potential negative effects allows them to avoid becoming victims.

Ability

Ability refers to the skills and capabilities of a worker. In some ways, ability is the most important advantage of autonomous employees because without it they would not be able to obtain or maintain the positions they occupy. Quite simply, they need to be able to perform their job tasks effectively and efficiently and that is not possible if ability is lacking.

The most common ability involves technical skills. Also known as hard skills, technical skills include math, science, reading, and writing abilities. Autonomous employees are typically among the best when it comes to technical skills. They use their ability to perform at peak levels and rarely need assistance from coworkers or managers to perform job tasks.

In many cases, the technical skills of autonomous employees are not limited to their area of expertise. For example, autonomous engineers possess mathematical skills, but they also skilled readers and writers. In combination, these abilities allow them to communicate and work with all types of employees; thereby making them even greater assets to the organizations that employ them.

Below are other important skills that autonomous employees bring to the table at their place of employment. Each of these skills has unique qualities that help organizations achieve goals and objectives. Unlike hard skills, they cannot all be learned in the classroom, but they often come naturally to autonomous employees.

Time management

Autonomous employees are organized and know how to manage their time properly. This ability is very important to leaders of organizations because time management is very difficult, if not impossible, for some workers. They simply cannot organize their time and efforts effectively and, without the help of direct supervision, fail to meet deadlines and fall behind on their jobs.

One important, but underrated, aspect of time management that is understood well by autonomous employees involves knowing when to give up. There comes a point where something is no longer worth investing time in and some employees are unable to recognize that point. Autonomous employees are able to see when something is simply not going to work so they pull the plug on it. This ability prevents time and money from being wasted and allows them to move on the matters that can be resolved.

Communication

Autonomous employees are typically good communicators with their coworkers and those higher up on the hierarchical ladder. This skill is important because interaction with others at all levels is needed for employees who strive to do the best job possible. Without good communication, information is lost in transition and misunderstanding occurs; thereby creating situations where people are unable to perform to the best of their abilities.

Autonomous employees are able to effectively communicate verbally, in writing, and sometimes even more importantly, non-verbally. They know their written and spoken words can impact people adversely so they are careful about what they write and say.   They also understand that their non-verbal actions often speak louder than their words and they are careful not to give off negative vibes to the people who work with and around them.

Resilience

No employee is perfect and they all experience failure. However, they do not all handle that failure the same. Some workers feel dejected and give up, some get mad and walk away, and others pick themselves up, dust themselves off, and try again. Autonomous employees fall into the third category because they are not afraid to give it another shot. They think about what they learned during their failed attempt and use that knowledge to make their next attempt a better one. They focus on their goals rather than their lack of accomplishments, and this often leads to them finding success when they try again.

Teamwork

Workplace teams are advantageous because every member can exchange thoughts and entertain other perspectives. Each employee has unique strengths that add diversity to the team, and the differing viewpoints contribute to the overall effectiveness. The synergy involved improves decision-making and helps the team reach goals within limited time frames.

Autonomous employees believe in the use of teams and they understand how to effectively function on them. They know teams utilize personnel to solve problems faster and more accurately than anyone can do alone. They also realize that every member of a team plays a role in the quest to achieve a goal and they understand the role that they need to play.

Comprehension

The most important skill in this list might be the ability of autonomous employees to comprehend the things that they need to learn for their jobs. Their minds function as sponges as they absorb relevant material decipher between what is important and what is not. This deciphering is a skill in itself because it prevents information that is not of significant value from causing confusion and clouding decision making.

The ability to comprehend is of great significance in the workplace. Without it, workers can get lost in a sea of information that becomes more and more confusing over time. Quite simply, employees who have trouble comprehending job-related information will have even more trouble being autonomous.

Leadership

Autonomous employees assume leadership roles in many different ways. They take ownership of their jobs by managing the everyday functions and interactions with coworkers. They are often viewed as authority figures by the people who work around them and their decisions are rarely questioned.

It is not uncommon for non-management personnel to take on specific aspects of leadership roles in organizations because people like to think of themselves as being in charge. However, it is rare that those people take responsibility for the mistakes they make, choosing instead to blame those mistakes on others. Autonomous employees function as leaders and make decisions, but they also take responsibility when those decisions are not the best.

Problem-solving

Problem-solving is a skill that all autonomous employees possess, and it requires them to use all of the resources that they have available. They need to gather facts, analyze data, research information, talk to people, and make decisions that lead to the accomplishment of goals and objectives.

Problem-solving is not a simple task, but autonomous employees are up to the challenge. They shift gears when necessary, read between the lines, and adjust when they need to do so. They are always searching for better answers and avoid using yesterday's solutions to solve today's problems. They are curious and ask why so they can look beyond the present and into the future for new ideas and solutions. In a nutshell, autonomous employees are true problem solvers...and they are highly valued for possessing this skill.

Summary

Autonomous employees have a significant impact on the organizations that employ them. They are flexible and change-oriented, innovative and modern, logical in their thought processes, committed to their jobs and organizations, aware of their surroundings, and adorned with many different skills and abilities

Unlike most of their coworkers, autonomous employees take ownership of their jobs and function as leaders for the work they perform. In this role, they make decisions that impact their work and the work of others, and they accept responsibility for those decisions.

This book discusses autonomous employees and their contributions to workplaces. It takes readers on a descriptive journey of their activities and shows how and why they are valued by organizational leaders. It is informational and educational, and it is written for easy understanding at all reader levels.

Congratulations! You now understand more about autonomous employees in leadership roles...workplace gems for managers in organizations.